BOY TO MAN

By Koby Sellings
Illustrated by Mila Aydingoz

We respect and honour Aboriginal and Torres Strait Islander Elders past, present and future. We acknowledge the stories, traditions and living cultures of Aboriginal and Torres Strait Islander peoples on this land and commit to building a brighter future together.

Library For All Ltd.

Young and strong Aboriginal boy,
whose family were from the mission.

He loved to sing, he loved to dance,
and he also loved his fishin'.

His favourite hobby was playing footy, and he loved to go to school.

He liked Physical Education class and Maths as well. His friends were pretty cool.

One day, he became the leader of his school, a smile he proudly wore.

That same year, he applied for Yalari. "I'm going to boarding school next year!" he swore.

And off to boarding school he went,
to learn and grow as he did.

Not without struggles along the way. But, from those struggles, he never hid.

He broke every barrier, he faced every challenge, all with a smile, of course.

19

Slowly this boy grew to be a man, and his voice became a powerful force.

The lessons he learned and the people
he met, built up his knowledge banks.

He became a man who's strong in himself, and there are many people he thanks.

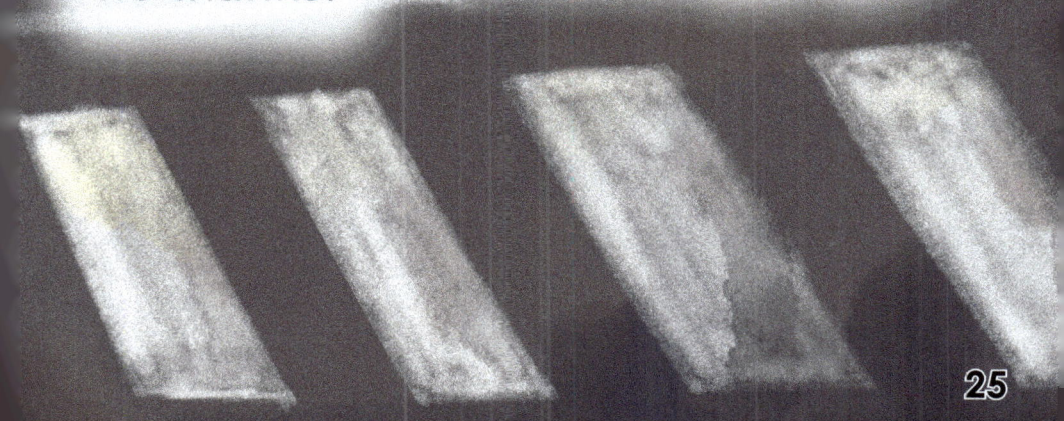

And now this man is on a journey,
one that means he can give back.

His heart is full, his spirits are high and, man, is he grateful for that.

You can use these questions to talk about this book with your family, friends and teachers.

What did you learn from this book?

Describe this book in one word. Funny? Scary? Colourful? Interesting?

How did this book make you feel when you finished reading it?

What was your favourite part of this book?

Download the Library For All Reader app from libraryforall.org

About the author

Koby Sellings is from Lakes Entrance (Gunaikurnai) and currently lives on Yugambeh land on the Gold Coast. He loves spending time with his family. As a child, he enjoyed the story of *Tiddalick*.

Darwin

NORTHERN
TERRITORY

QUEENSLAND

WESTERN
AUSTRALIA

SOUTH
AUSTRALIA

Brisbane

NEW SOUTH
WALES

Perth

Adelaide

Sydney

ACT
Canberra

VICTORIA
Melbourne

Author's Country

TASMANIA
Hobart

Our Yarning

The Our Yarning collection aligns with the Australian Curriculum through the Cross-Curriculum Priorities — Aboriginal and Torres Strait Islander Histories and Cultures. The collection provides an authentic opportunity for learning and embedding Aboriginal and Torres Strait Islander perspectives because it is written by Aboriginal and Torres Strait Islander people.

We know that children learn better, and enjoy reading more, when they see themselves in the stories, characters and illustrations of the books they read.

To download the app, visit the Google Play Store or Apple Store and search 'Our Yarning'.

libr021foral1.org

You're reading Level 4

Learner – Beginner readers

Start your reading journey with short words, big ideas and plenty of pictures.

Level 1 – Rising readers

Raise your reading level with more words, simple sentences and exciting images.

Level 2 – Eager readers

Enjoy your reading time with familiar words, but complex sentences.

Level 3 – Progressing readers

Develop your reading skills with creative stories and some challenging vocabulary.

Level 4 – Fluent readers

Step up your reading skills with playful narratives, new words and fun facts.

Middle Primary – Curious readers

Discover your world through science and stories.

Upper Primary – Adventurous readers

Explore your world through science and stories.

Boy to Man

First published 2025

Published by Library For All Ltd
Email: info@libraryforall.org
URL: libraryforall.org

Our Yarning logo design by Jason Lee, Bidjipidji Art

Original illustrations by Mila Aydingoz

Boy to Man
Sellings, Koby
ISBN: 978-1-923429-87-1
SKU04638

www.ingramcontent.com/pod-product-compliance
Lightning Source LLC
Chambersburg PA
CBHW042340040426
42448CB00019B/3352